food

pastime

animal

book

comfort

aversion

WHAT ARE YOU LIKE?

transport

place

shoes

weather

clothes

music

possession

SELF-REVEALING ARTWORKS BY PEOPLE IN THE PUBLIC EYE · FOREWORD BY QUENTIN BLAKE

First published 2008
by House of Illustration
16 Lincoln's Inn Fields
WC2A 3ED
www.houseofillustration.org.uk
© House of Illustration
All works © the artists
Designed by BOB Design

We would like to thank the John Brown Trust
for its support in facilitating this publication.

ISBN 978-0-955946-0-9
Distributed by Network Books
42 Spencer Rise
London NW5 1AP

CONTENTS

I remember once being asked by my editor, in a public interview at some French book fair or other, what I felt about the constraints of illustration; and my responding, with perhaps a hint of bravura, that I really liked them. So I do, though I am ready to confess that it is not always quite as simple as that. I don't imagine, for instance, that the production of two small drawings an inch by an inch-and-a-half, within an hour and a half once a week, for the letters page of a Sunday paper — my task for a year or so earlier in life — added much to the imaginative enlargement of my work, even though a need for selection and concision made its own demands.

Nevertheless the old idea that illustration is a form essentially disabled by commercial considerations is a false one, and the constraints of size and shape, method of production, number of images and, most of all, of situation and narrative can be what drives the artist on: stimulates imagination and gives it form and order. Pressing against constraints may, indeed, be part of the process, but I have no doubt that it is possible and delightful to work within them and create work that is idiosyncratic and personal.

And this is what I believe the forty-five contributors to this book, and the exhibition of which it is the outcome, have done. In one sense it is just a game, but we only invited those whom we thought would bring to it an appropriate degree of visual expertise. Almost without exception they agreed to take part. Many are not artist-illustrators; some are painters or designers; some have had artistic training but are now writers, critics, musicians; and there are others (like Andrew Marr and Anna Ford) who, though without artistic training and not professional artists, produce art and take it seriously.

Certainly it was gratifying to notice how seriously everyone, including the most light-hearted, took the task, and to see what a wonderful diversity of approach and technique ensued; from the classic answer of David Gentleman, for instance, with everything lucidly balanced and beautifully drawn, through the elegant design of Jeff Fisher, the sharply observed notation of Posy Simmonds, to those who ingeniously cheated (can we say that, when ingenuity can be a real part of the game?) such as David Shrigley, who based his whole response on an assumed consuming passion for snakes (unless, in which case apologies, this is the truth) or Nick Garland, who, finding he had more favourite aversions than he could well deal with, carried out the task in exemplary fashion by writing the letter (q.v.)

which explains in detail how he couldn't possibly do it. Perhaps strangely only one artist, Steven Appleby, used the prospect of anonymity deliberately to mislead, and offered himself another identity as a mystery woman of exotic tastes.

This is only a hint of the assortment of flavours; and needless to say the most eloquent expression of forty-five diverse personalities is not simply in the objects they have chosen but in the ways that they have chosen to depict them.

What Are You Like?, like the book and exhibition In All Directions, which was about illustration and travel and organised with the Arts Council, anticipates, and contributes to, the opening of a new home and centre for illustration in the great new King's Cross re-development. When within a few years that happens, we look forward to a programme of exhibitions and publications which explore and display the rich past, present and possible future of this extraordinary world of images: so much part of our everyday lives yet at the same time often little known about.

The debt of gratitude we owe to the artists in this book goes beyond the work that they have put into their contributions, because each of them has generously granted us permission to preserve their work in our museum archive; a striking gesture of support for our venture. Perhaps we should even emulate the self-portrait scheme of the Uffizi and invite all our future exhibiting artists to leave their visual expression of What They Are Like?

Quentin Blake

P.S. What Are You Like? was arranged, organised and brought to completion by Claudia Zeff. She has also been a wire of energy and determination that has run through the House of Illustration project from its very beginnings, and I offer her my bouquet.

NICK GARLAND
born in London 1935, brought up in
New Zealand and a political cartoonist
on the Daily Telegraph since 1966.

6 December 2007

Dear Quentin,
    Your letter presented me with a difficulty. I wanted to take part in the game you proposed but I am unable to identify favourites.
    I cannot say that I prefer a tiger to an elephant or Chekhov to Varlam Shalamov. I have scores of aversions. They include forced laughter, and TV announcers who emphasise the wrong words: "The bomb went off IN Baghdad..." I don't like the idiotic phrase "breaking news" either.
    Of course I understood that this is a game, but it is not one I can play. I keep thinking "If I say drawing is my favourite pastime what about playing with a grandchild?" And then what about drawing with a grandchild?
    Favourite possession? Impossible to say. The old Parker Fountain pen that I'm writing with now - or a small sand stone that I bought in India from a poor man who was sitting by the road carving odd little objects out of yellow stone and selling them for about 2 farthings each. He gave me the beautiful Ganesh and said something. I asked my companion to translate. "He said, 'This is my Ganesh!" I have puzzled ever since. Did he mean "Ganesh is my God" or "This is how I see Ganesh" or "I am selling you my beloved carving of Ganesh"?
    I paid him more than he asked for so he threw in a stone butterfly and a stone fish. I've got about 100 favourite possessions. As for clothes...
    There is a pleasure in dressing up smartly. I have a black linen suit that I like wearing but I like jeans too and kimonos*

* This is not a kimono - it is a Yukata. Kimonos are for outdoors

Is it possible to say you have favourite music? NO - it isn't. Sometimes Mozart will blow you away sometimes Bob Dylan and sometimes Bing Crosby... and Beethoven and Chopin and Steve Earle...

ME LOOKING FOR A FAVOURITE PLACE

weather? who knows.

I do have a favourite film. It is "The Third Man" I have seen it over and over again; and a favourite caricaturist — Richard Winnington — whose drawings of Orson Welles I copied when I was a child. Copying Richard Winnington made me want to be a cartoonist.

Yours ever, Nick Garland

KOLYMA TALES VARLAM SHALAMOV

BREAKING NEWS

Ganesh

7

ANIMAL

COMFORT

PASTIME

PLACE

POS

OD

TRANSPORT

ESSION

WEATHER

MARY FEDDEN
was born in Bristol in 1915, and for fifty years has lived and worked in her riverside studio at Hammersmith.

ANDREW MARR
is a BBC television and radio presenter, writer and poorish amateur artist: and a child inside his head.

Wester ~~Ross is~~
My favourite place

3.

A painting by
Gillian Ayres is m
favourite possession

4.

My favourite comfort
is malt whisky
from Islay.

JEFF FISHER (LEFT)
has, with his own hands, produced over
1000 book jackets. He lives in France.

POSY SIMMONDS (ABOVE)
draws and writes newspaper cartoons,
graphic novels and children's books.

my favorite food
Honey

my favorite
dislike
smoking

my

my favorite profession
if I were not
an artist chef

my favorite artist
paul Klee

my fa
Indr

te pastime

my favorite books

Günter DIE
Grass
BLECH!
TROMMEL

Slaughter
House
5

Vonnegut Kurt

Composer
Beethoven

my favorite drink

orange
juice

ERIC CARLE
has created more than
70 books for children including
The Very Hungry Caterpillar.

15

QUENTIN BLAKE
has illustrated 300 books, was the
first Children's Laureate, and lives
in London and France.

Favourite 1 Transport: Bicyc
2 Place: Beach

Food: Bacon Sandwich   5 Comfort: Scarves   7 Footwear: Trainers
Animal: I don't know   6 Book: Alphonse Allais   8 Weather: Breezy
what this is

RODNEY FITCH (ABOVE)
works all over the world running
Fitch, one of the world's largest
design firms.

PETER CAMPBELL (RIGHT)
a typographer, also writes and
draws for the London Review of Books.

18

19

BRIAN ENO
is a composer, producer and artist.

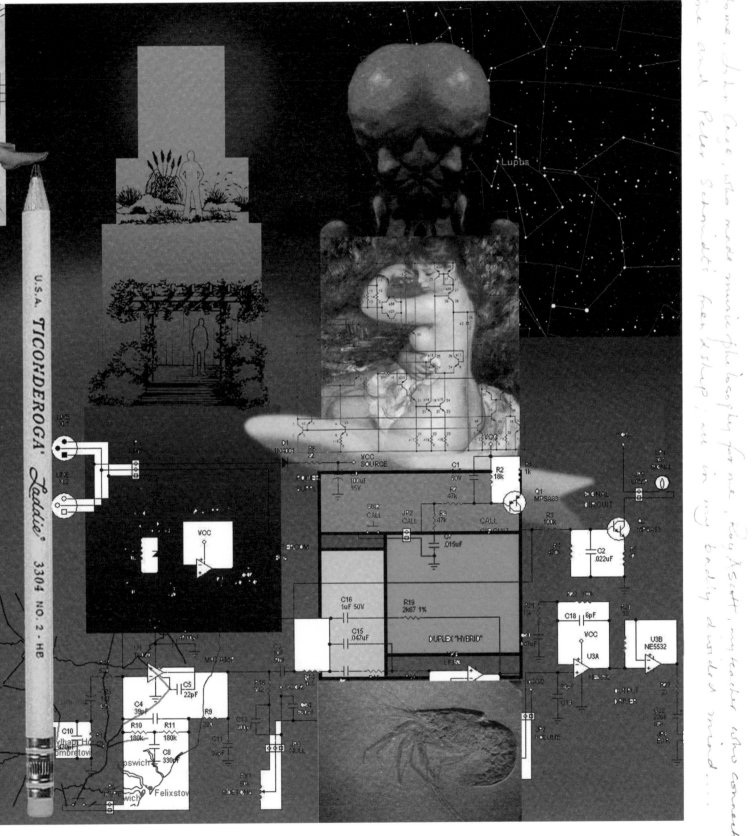

bonds of flesh, Richard Rorty, the philosopher who made philosophy

t diagrams of synthesizers, fossils, my early companions, space and

the soft breeze, the sea of light spun from afar: deck of Professor Geography

21

STEVEN APPLEBY
has written and drawn for
newspapers, books, radio,
television and even the stage.

favourite shoes

favourite comfort

pet aversion

WHO AM I?

favourite book

Help...
I don't know
anymore.

THE LAKE

High hills

November 2007

Dearest Nicolette — howareyou?

I'm glad IN A WAY that's you've asked me that Question? It's made me really have to THINK and that's NO BAD thing!

FAVOURITE things

Now there..... here...
You were with me buying those CRAZY a bit RASH as it turns out - I can only wear them for a MAX 5 MINS before its OUCH! PULSE its RARE for me to go anywhere without my

AND the mini best friend

Are you still wearing my favourite

This is my kind of weather. Towers of cream sailing in blue

BUT today it's

So to lift my SPIRITS, I'll pick up and pluck whilst dreaming of SWAYING

in whispering palms

uke cannot be serious

COME SOON & WE'LL MUNCH

I miss you x x darling x

1. Place - Mount Olympus   2. Shoe - Nike Sabaku Samurai   3. Possession - Ancient Goddess Head   4. Weather - Rain

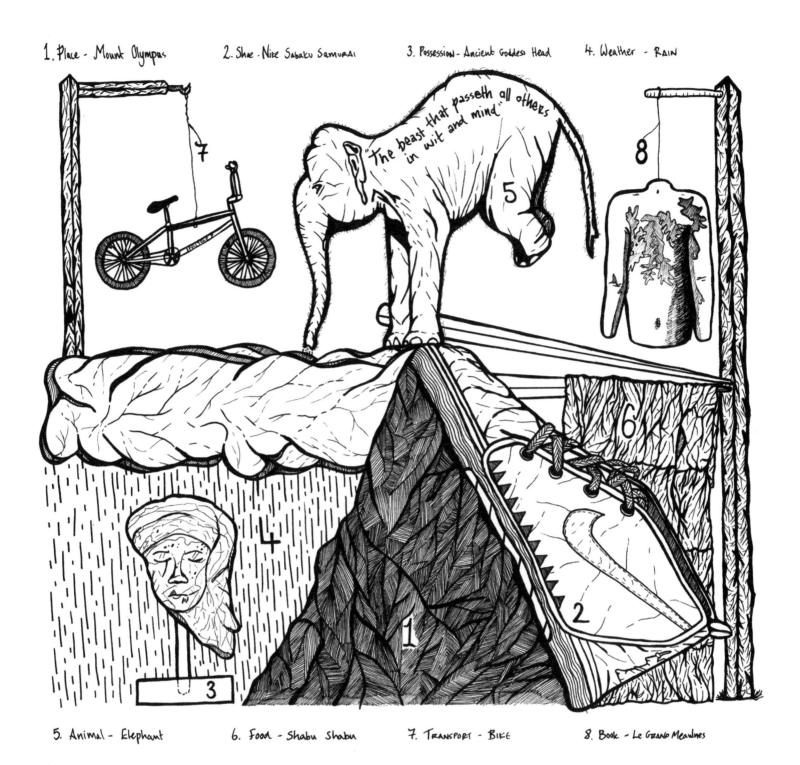

"The beast that passeth all others in wit and mind"

5. Animal - Elephant   6. Food - Shabu Shabu   7. Transport - Bike   8. Book - Le Grand Meaulnes

GEORGINA VON ETZDORF (LEFT)
is an internationally renowned textile designer, famous for rhythm in design, inspirational colour, and sensual textures.

JACK PENATE (ABOVE)
is a London-born 23 year-old musician who is currently writing his second record.

25

EMMA CHICHESTER CLARK
has written and illustrated many
children's books and lives by the
river in London.

Displayed below, you will find a f

comfort · pastime · transport

aversion · possession · animal · music · book · weather

FAVOURITE

city – London

weather – Fog

bridge – Hammersmith

bus – Routemaster

coppers – Mounted Police

event – Boat Race

colour – Light Blue

dog – Bridge

bantams – Nigel, Zuleika & Cara

JAN PIENKOWSKI
arrived London age 9; read Classics
Cambridge; done art everywhere
ever since.

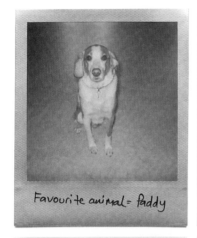

Favourite animal = Paddy

Favourite possession = paperweights

My Favourite clothes

Favourite pastime

Favourite Mode of transport

Favourite place = Bed.

Favourite Weather Today

Favourite shoes

MARY McCARTNEY (ABOVE)
is a renowned portrait and fashion photographer. Her work has been published and exhibited worldwide.

PHILIP PULLMAN (RIGHT)
was born in 1946. He has published over twenty novels. In 2005 he was awarded the Astrid Lindgren Memorial Award.

30

My favourite hands
Jude's

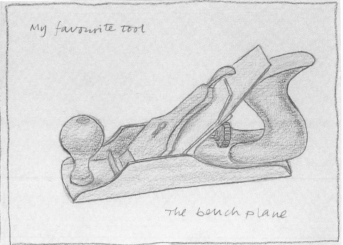

The bench plane

My favourite form of transport

The Rocking Horse

My favourite musical instrument

The ukulele

My favourite place

Portmeirion

My favourite characters in fiction

ZIP

Krazy Kat and Ignatz Mouse

My favourite food

DRIPPING

Toast & dripping

My favourite shoes

31

3

6

Childhood cat, Mickey

1

Writing Home
Alan Bennett
the number one bestseller
new 1997 edition with additional material

2

7

"There's no such thing as bad weather, only inadequate clothing." ...Ted Hughes

10

MARGARET HOWELL
has designed clothes since 1970.
Today her shops also promote
British design she admires.
She is based in London.

5

8

Buy 2
For £5

BUT
NOT OUT OF
SEASON OR
OUT OF PACKETS

Raspberries by air
Fragrantly sweet and tangy

1
5-a-day
= 25 raspberries

Display until
29 NOV
Best before
30 NOV

Produce of
MEXICO
Weight
260g e

4

KEY
1 Animal
2 Book
3 Clothes
4 Food
4 Aversion
5 Transport
6 Music
7 Pastime
8 Place
9 Shoes
10 Weather

Favourite – in season   Aversion – out of season

LAURA CARLIN
works as a freelance illustrator in
London. She mainly draws abuse and
finds happy subjects very difficult
to deal with.

WILLIAM FEAVER
is a painter, writer, curator, critic who
lives in London and Northumberland.

36

favourite place: Allendale in all weathers

favourite animal & comfort: whippet

favourite shoes a transport: walking boots

My Favourites — Animal — dinosaur. Transport — a woman's arms. Book — The Wi
Food — raw carrots. Place — beside the sea. Music — the sound of the sea. Pastime — Bea
Weather — bright blue day. Comfort — a cat. Footwear — Converse. Clothing — blue

e Willows.
all.

To ride in a woman's arms
on a dinosaur with Toad and Ratty
and a Cat eating carrots
on a bright blue day
by the Sea = A GOOD DAY OUT.

MICHEAL FOREMAN
has illustrated a vast range of books
for both children and adults for which
he has won many awards.

DAVID GENTLEMAN
is an artist and designer.
He lives in London.

My favourite clothes and shoes

My favourite weather

My favourite form of transport

40

My favourite possession

My pet aversion

My favourite animal

My favourite place

My favourite comfort

My favourite food

PAUL SMITH
is from Nottingham and
wanted to be a cyclist but
is now a fashion designer.

the milky way : full moon : cats : ancient trees : daydreaming : books :   wild flowers   swimming : flowers : mountains : storms : icebergs : sku : birds :

ANNA FORD (ABOVE)
has been drawing most of her life
and illustrated a book for her friend
Mary Fedden.

PETER CAPALDI (RIGHT)
is an actor, writer and director
who lives in London with his wife
and daughter.

1. Pastime: cinema
2. Place: home
3. Weather: stormy
4. Food: pasta
5. Clothes: 18th Century
6. Comfort: wine
7. Shoes: brothel creepers
8. Music: David Bowie

SHIRLEY HUGHES
has written and illustrated 60 books.
In 2007 Dogger won the Greenaway
of Greenaways award.

① Animal : cat ② Book: 'Our Mutual Fr

④ Food: a picnic with plenty of fruit ⑤ Past

⑧ Shoes: green suede lace-ups ⑨ W

y Charles Dickens ③ Clothes: wide brimmed hat, jacket with pockets.

awing out of doors ⑥ Place: Sussex Downs ⑦ Possession: 'Dogger'

: sunny but not too hot ⑩ Pet Aversion: dead birds

ERIC CLAPTON (ABOVE)
was born in 1945 and is a world-
renowned guitarist and composer
of popular music works.

BRUCE INGMAN (RIGHT)
trained at the RCA. His award-winning
books have been described as 'dazzling'
and 'ravishingly elegant'.

48

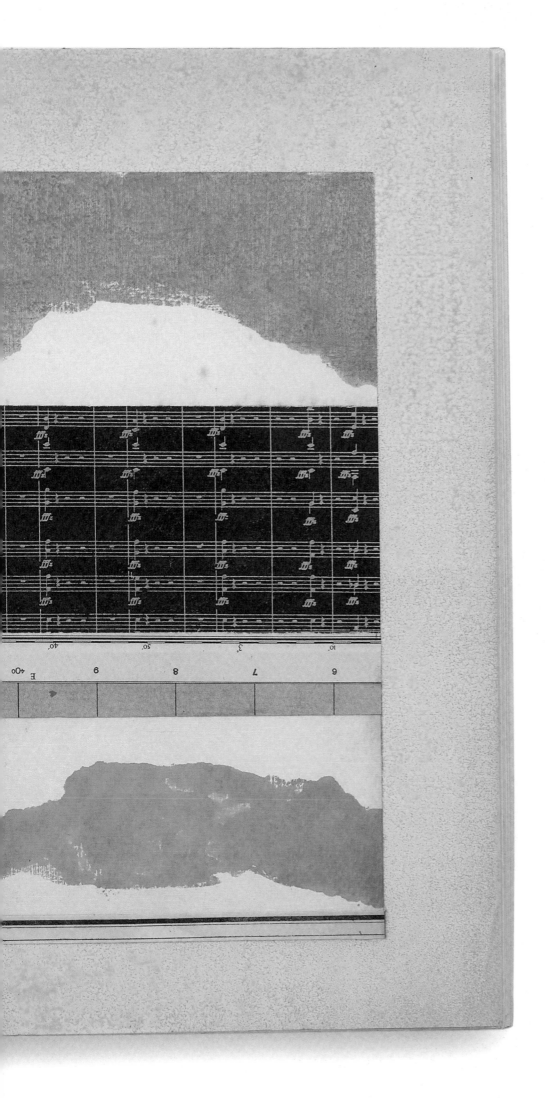

DAN FERN
is an artist and teacher. He believes
that music is the true internet.

DAVID ADJAYE (ABOVE)
is the Principal of Adjaye Associates,
an international architectural practice.

JOE BERGER (RIGHT)
is an illustrator and cartoonist.
His first children's book, Bridget
Fidget, is out now.

LAUREN CHILD
sort of became a children's author-illustrator by accident and has worked on about 30 books.

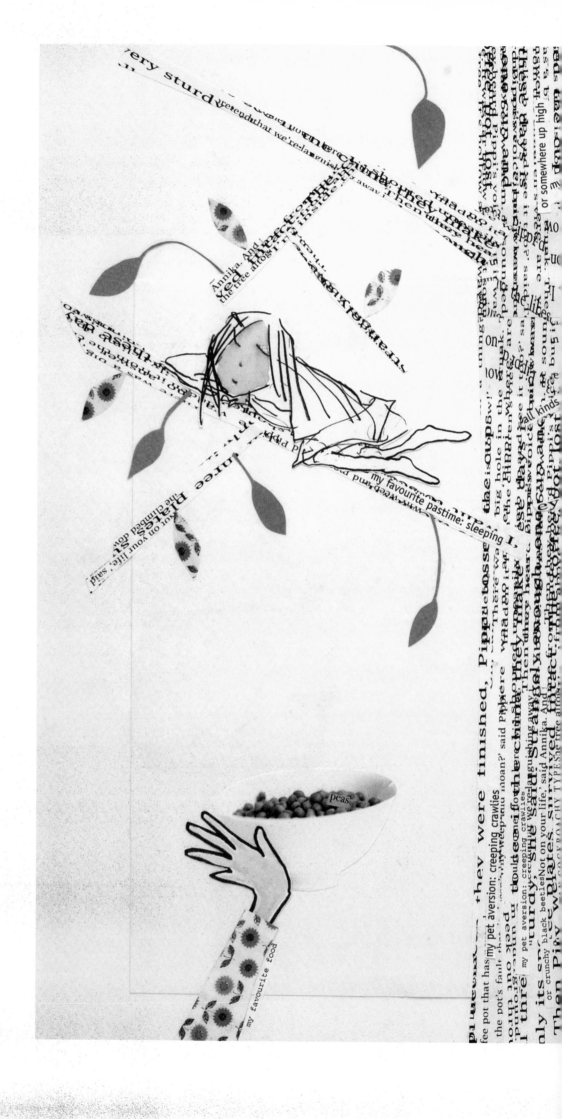

1 TRANSPORT (INTER CITY)
2 MUSIC (THEREMIN)
3 COMFORT (CENTRAL HEATING)
4 BOOK (HOW TO BE PERFECT by RON PADGETT)

5 PET AVERSION (EXAMS)
6 FOOD (TOFU)
7 SHOES (CASUAL)
8 PLACE (NUTWOOD)

GLEN BAXTER
was born in Leeds but following
an unfortunate brush with
chiaroscuro now finds himself
inexplicably in London.

MINI GREY

born unexpectedly in a car park, her
chequered career has culminated in
making picture books.

WENDY RAMSHAW
exhibits internationally,
her work is in over 70 museums
and public collections.

MY FAVOURITE ANIMAL IS A CAT • MY FAVORITE BOOK IS ALICE • MY FAVO
MY FAVORITE PASTIME IS READING. • MY PLACE IS THE SEA • ONE OF MY
FAVORITE.

MFORT IS A CUP OF TEA • MY FAVORITE FOOD IS CHOCOLATE — SEE CAKE •

POSSESIONS IS A RING • MY FAVORITE SHOES ARE BOOTS • AND I AM NO GOOD AT SPELLING •

WILLIAM PACKER (ABOVE)
was first a painter, became a
critic by chance, and still wears
both hats.

DAVID SHRIGLEY (RIGHT)
makes drawings, sculpture, photo-
graphs, animations and sometimes
writes songs. He lives in Glasgow.

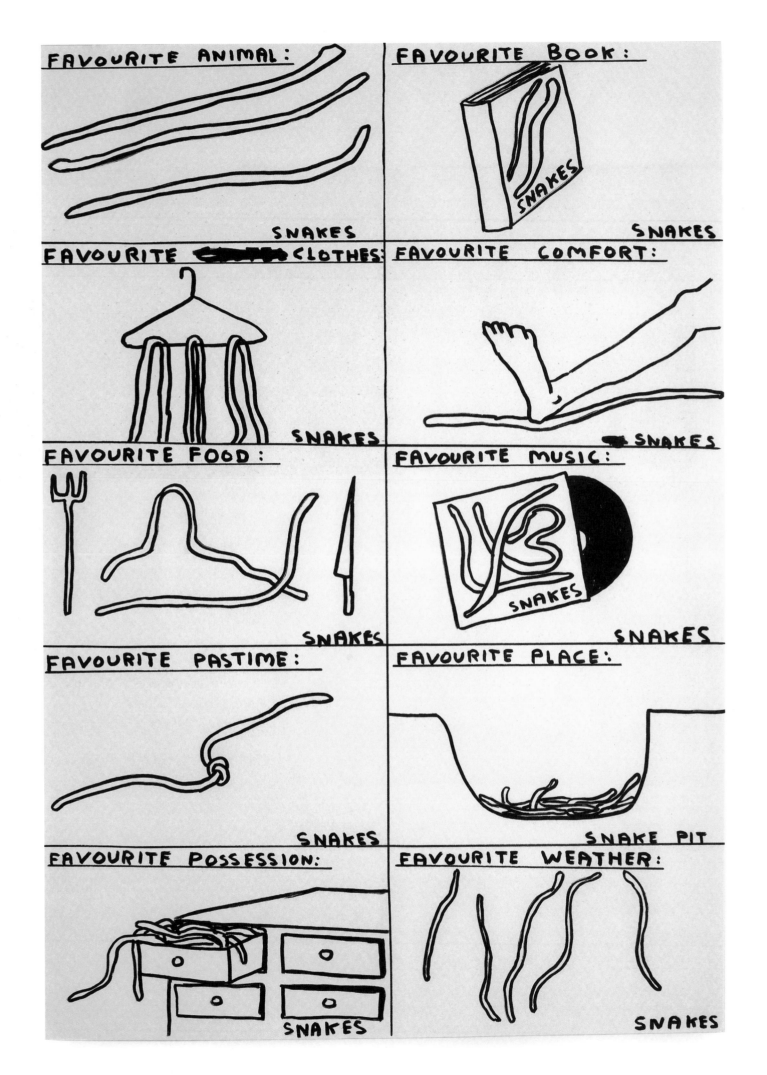

FAVOURITE ANIMAL:

SNAKES

FAVOURITE BOOK:

SNAKES

FAVOURITE ~~CLOTHES:~~ CLOTHES:

SNAKES

FAVOURITE COMFORT:

SNAKES

FAVOURITE FOOD:

SNAKES

FAVOURITE MUSIC:

SNAKES

FAVOURITE PASTIME:

SNAKES

FAVOURITE PLACE:

SNAKE PIT

FAVOURITE POSSESSION:

SNAKES

FAVOURITE WEATHER:

SNAKES

MARION DEUCHARS
London based, has worked on projects from Formula One to Jamie Oliver's cookbook.

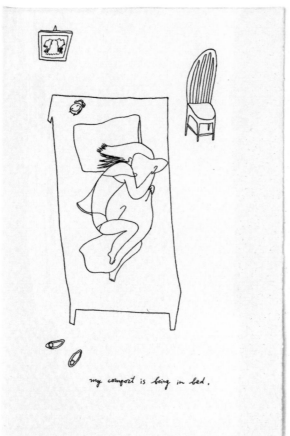

my comfort is being in bed.

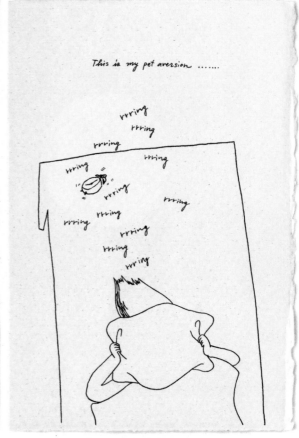

My favorite clothes is
My old jeans.

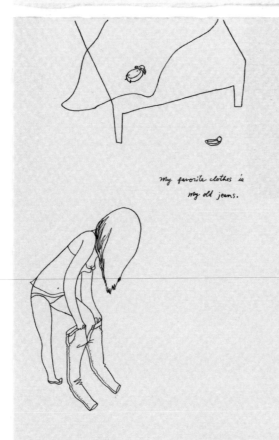

I have lots of
favorite shoes.

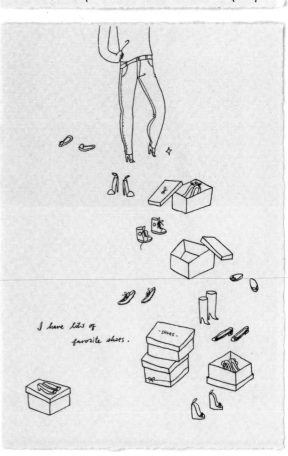

66

MIO MATSUMOTO
gets inspiration from her daily life
and has illustrated in various fields.
She lives in Japan.

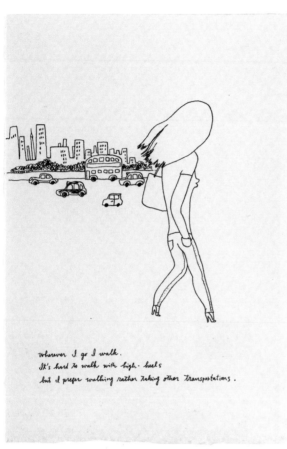

wherever I go I walk.
It's hard to walk with high-heels
but I prefer walking rather taking other transportations.

park is a good place to walk.

And may be lie down and read
my favorite book.
"The little prince".

As there is a chance to see a rainbow,
I like when it's raining.

67

Russell Mills: What Are You Like? Favourites
1. Music: Arvo Pärt (Black Grey Gold) 2. Pastime: Reading (texts)   3. Possession: Imagination   4. Book: The Life and Opinions of
Tristram Shandy Gentleman

5. Place: Under Loughrigg, Rydal   6. Weather: Autumnal   7. Comforts: Gitanes + Guinness   8. Animal: Bull Terrier
                                                                    Cigs   (Stains)

RUSSELL MILLS
is a multimedia artist who lives
and works in Ambleside, Cumbria.

JOANNA CAREY
has worked as an art teacher for many years, and writes about illustration.

MY FAVOURITE:

1. <u>ANIMAL</u>

MY *favourite* DOG:

<u>Bubu</u>

2. <u>BOOK</u>

" IS what you <u>see</u> always
BEHIND *you*? "

" Journeys

TO RECOVER   TO RELIVE
your FUTURE   YOUR *past* "

3. CLOTHES

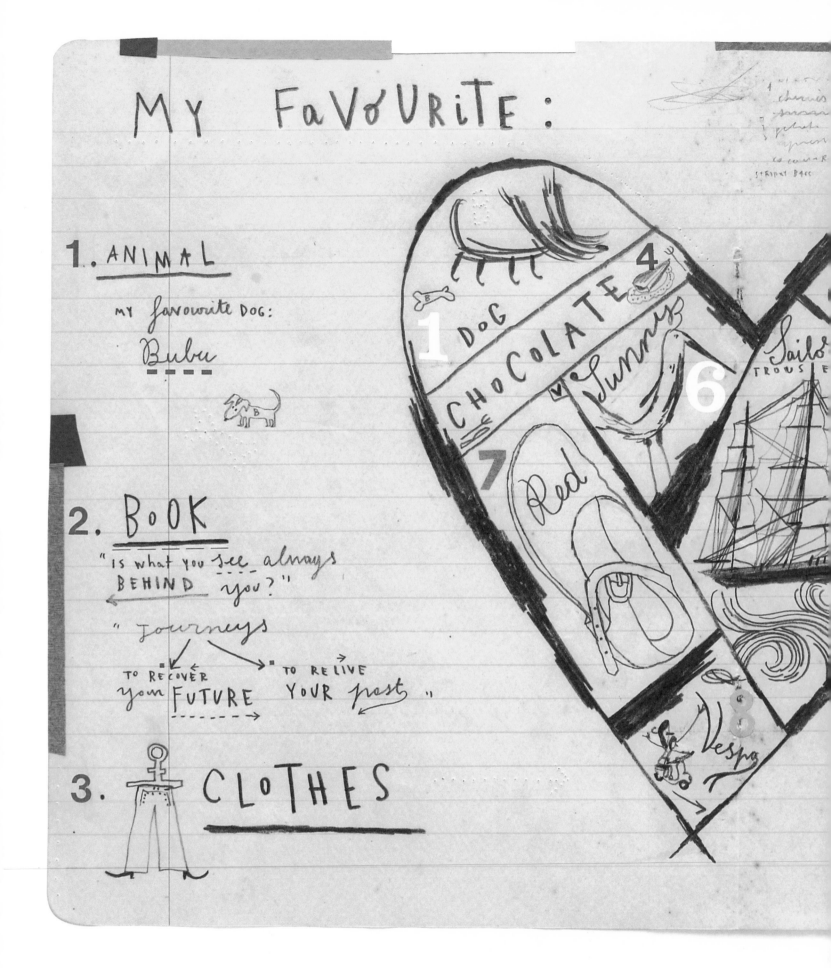

1 DOG

CHOCOLATE 4

Sunny

Sailo
TROUSE

6

7

Red

8

Vespa

SARA FANELLI
born in Italy, she now works in London.
She has illustrated stamps, covers,
posters and children's books.

4. FOOD

my FAVOURITE
FORM of chocolate:
CHOCOLATE CAKE → (moist !)

5. PLACE
(20 July 196)

6. WEATHER
HOT
SUMMER

7. SHOES

8. FORM OF TRANSPORT
(back of ....)

FAVOURITE ANIMAL...

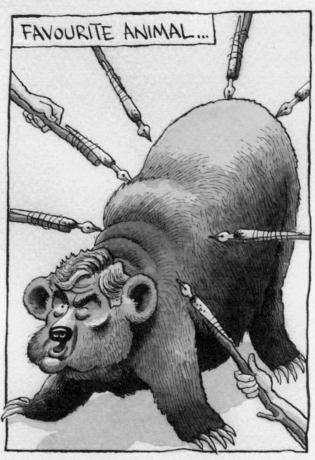

PASTIME...

MUSIC...

BOOK...

GREAT EXPECTATIONS

WEATHER...

SHOES...

FOOD...

S.N.PARP

PET AVERSION...

PETER BROOKES
is the political cartoonist of The Times
and draws covers for The Spectator.

PETER BLAKE
born Dartford in 1932, RCA, RDI-
Professor of Drawing. Lives and
works in London.

THESE ARE A FEW OF MY FAVOURITE THINGS

WHAT A

Animal
Cheeta

Cheeta at his 75th birthday pa

Food
The pie

MARKS & SPENCER
Medium Pork Pie
Rich pastry filled with seasoned
cured pork   145 g
22 APR

Form of transpo
Trains

Possession
Tom Thumb's boots

Shoes
Dorothy's

RE YOU LIKE ?

Book	Clothes	Comfort
e Great Gatsby	Black linen suit	Cashmere

Music	Pastime	Place
Brian Wilson	Painting	London

Weather	Aversion	Mottos
utumn sunshine	Rats	

Living well is the best revenge.

Staying ahead of the Avant-Garde.

my favourites

place: the sky

animal

shoes

RIP

Greyfriars Bobby

high heels

comfor

alcohol

pastime and music

singing

book: Gentlemen Prefer Blondes

by Anit

Lo

DONALD URQUHART
is a Scottish artist, writer and
performer who is based in London.

weather

dramatic
thunderstorms

transport

Roller Coaster

food : beetroot

chutney

raw

soup

salad

cooked

pickled

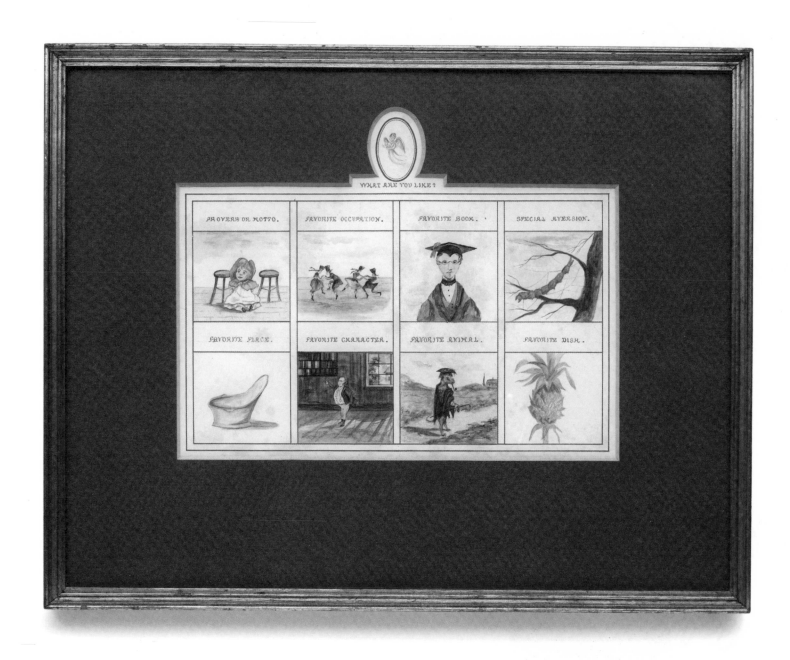

The original Victorian
What Are You Like?
Artist unknown.